Presented To:

_____

Presented By:

_____

Date:

From a
Friend's
Heart

NELSON BOOKS
A Division of Thomas Nelson Publishers
Since 1798

www.thomasnelson.com

Published in Nashville, Tennessee, by Thomas Nelson, Inc.

Nelson Books titles may be purchased in bulk for educational, business, fund-raising, or sales promotional use. For information, please e-mail SpecialMarkets@ThomasNelson.com.

Scripture quotations noted NKJV are from The New King James Version®. Copyright ©1979, 1980, 1982 by Thomas Nelson, Inc. Used by permission. All rights reserved.

Scripture quotations noted CEV are from The Contemporary English Version. Copyright © 1991, 1992, 1995 by American Bible Society. Used by permission.

Scripture quotations noted MSG are from The Message. Copyright © by Eugene H. Peterson 1993, 1994, 1995. Used by permission of NavPress Publishing Group.

Scripture quotations noted NIV are from the Holy Bible: New International Version®. Copyright © 1973, 1978, 1984 by International Bible Society. Used by permission of Zondervan Publishing House. All rights reserved.

Scripture quotations noted NLT are from the Holy Bible, New Living Translation, copyright © 1996. Used by permission of Tyndale House Publishers, Inc., Wheaton, Illinois 60189. All rights reserved.

Scripture quotations noted NRSV are from The New Revised Standard Version of the Bible. Copyright © 1989 by the Division of Christian Education of the National Council of The Churches of Christ in the U.S.A. All rights reserved.

Managing Editor: Lila Empson
Associate Editor: Kyle L. Olund
Manuscript: Candy Paull
Design: Whisner Design Group, Tulsa, Oklahoma

Library of Congress Cataloging-in-Publication Data

From a friend's heart : 50 reflections on living well.
    p. cm.
  ISBN 0-7852-1477-1 (pbk.)
  1. Friendship--Religious aspects--Christianity--Meditations. 2.
Christian life--Meditations.
  BV4647.F7F76 2005
  241'.6762--dc22

2005028178

Printed in the United States of America

06 07 08 09 QW 5 4 3 2 1

Optimism is the faith that leads to achievement.
Nothing can be done without hope and confidence.

Helen Keller

Contents

Introduction

True friendship—one of the greatest gifts life offers—is nurtured in the rich soil of mutual appreciation and compassionate understanding. Friends create and share common memories. No matter how far apart they live, they are united by a heritage of love and laughter. Friends cry on each other's shoulders, stand together in hard times, laugh over silly jokes, and share solemn secrets.

> Friends are the sunshine of life.
>
> John Hay

A friend can be the buddy you hang out with as well as the one who is closest to your heart. Friends dream together and share in the most important moments of life. May this little book of friendly advice and spiritual wisdom remind you of the friend who loves you dearly and wishes only the best for you all the days of your life.

May God be merciful and bless us.
May his face shine with favor upon us.

Psalm 67:1 NLT

9

Follow your heart, and it will lead you where you need to go.

All that is worth cherishing in this world begins with the heart.

The heart is wiser than the head. Though you need to pay attention to the logic of the mind, the wisdom of the heart guides you most surely when it comes to the most important choices in life. The logical choice in a career might seem to be the job that pays the most money, but you'll find more satisfaction in doing something you love, even when it might mean less money. Faced with a choice between love and logic, let love be the deciding factor. The money will follow. When you let love lead the way, you'll discover that you've tapped into God's higher wisdom. God is love, and when you make choices out of love, you align yourself with his priorities. Trust love to lead you in the right direction.

> We are shaped and fashioned by what we love.
>
> Wolfgang von Goethe

Above all else, guard your heart, for it is the wellspring of life.

Proverbs 4:23 NIV

Expressing gratitude deepens your joy in the gifts of life.

Count your blessings and watch them multiply.

Growing up, you were taught to say thank you. Though you might have merely imitated grown-up good manners at first, giving thanks became an important ritual. Whether it was thanking a date for a good time or a friend for a much-appreciated birthday present, polite gratitude became second nature. Giving thanks and expressing gratitude are even more important now that you're older. Sincere appreciation creates a circle of giving, where both giver and receiver share in the joy of giving. Expressing gratitude enhances your enjoyment of the gift and deepens the pleasure for the giver. Whether you are thanking someone for offering a helping hand or praising God for a beautiful day, gratitude sincerely expressed makes a gift received even more precious.

> Gratitude is the memory of the heart.
>
> J. B. Massieu

I will sing to the LORD as long as I live.
I will praise my God to my last breath!

Psalm 104:33 NLT

Those who bring sunshine to others cannot keep it from themselves.

A friend's smile and laughter can light up the world.

Your caring touch and warm smile light up the lives of others. Your smile lights up your face and brings sunshine to everyone around you. If a friend's eyes are clouded with tears, your tender hug and loving understanding can drive the storm clouds away. Because you care, you are a comfort to friends, family, and even to strangers. When you spread the sunshine of God's love, some of those heartwarming sunbeams smile back on you. Your decision to look on the sunny side of life helps others in ways you may not understand, but God will pass the love and hope along. Let joy light your heart, and may you share the love of God as freely as sunshine.

Joy is the holy fire that keeps our purpose warm and our intelligence aglow.

Helen Keller

Happy indeed are those whose God is the LORD.

Psalm 144:15 NLT

Friends share a love that can be divided endlessly and still not diminish.

With friends there is always plenty of love to go around.

Love is not a commodity to be hoarded; love is a blessing to be shared. When you are rooted deeply in God's love, you have access to a boundless supply of energy, joy, hope, and peace. The more love you give away, the more God gives to you, and the more love there is to go around. Like a tree that is planted beside the river of life, grow in God's love. Be generous with your heart and offer others compassion instead of judgment, kindness instead of indifference, and encouragement instead of criticism. Give your love freely, allowing God to bring love full circle around to you again, in His own time and in His own way. Share your love freely, knowing God is your supply.

Love is a fruit in season at all times, and within the reach of every hand.

Mother Teresa

Anyone who holds on to life just as it is destroys that life. But if you let it go, reckless in your love, you'll have it forever, real and eternal.

John 12:25 MSG

Forgiveness is a gift you give to yourself as well as to the person you forgive.

When you know how to forgive fully, you know how to live fully.

One of the most important life lessons you learn is how to practice the art of forgiveness. When a friendly squabble turns into hasty words, what is said may not be forgotten. But what is said can be forgiven. Those childhood apologies and lessons in forgiveness are even more important in adulthood. People say and do hurtful things that can't be unsaid or undone. But with God's grace, they can be forgiven. When you choose to forgive, you give a great gift to yourself as well as to the other person. You give the gift of freedom. No longer bound by the past, your choice to forgive opens a door to the future. When you forgive others, you open your heart to God's love and create a place for healing to begin.

> Forgiveness saves the expense of anger, the cost of hatred, the waste of spirits.
>
> Hannah More

Blessed are the merciful, for they shall obtain mercy.

Matthew 5:7 NKJV

*When you emphasize what you have
in common with others, you'll enjoy
the differences more.*

*Friends are free to celebrate their
differences as well as their
common heritage.*

Sometimes friends are very different. One friend enjoys sports and feels comfortable only in jeans. Another friend loves Victorian lace and formal tea parties. One loves books; another loves fast cars. Yet it is the differences that make life more interesting—and fun. God made each person unique. You may have to work a little harder to find common ground with those who have different tastes, interests, and outlooks on life, but those very differences enrich you and broaden your outlook on life. Whether it's family, friends, or people you've just met, look for what you have in common. Everyone wants to be loved and appreciated. Emphasize the love you have in common, and you'll be more likely to appreciate the differences.

Be kind. Remember that everyone you meet is fighting a hard battle.

Harry Thompson

Let us pursue the things which make for peace and the things by which one may edify another.

Romans 14:19 NKJV

Faced with a choice between love and logic,
let love be the deciding factor.

The more love you give away, the
more God gives to you, and the
more love there is to go around.

When you spread the sunshine of God's
love, some of those heartwarming
sunbeams smile back on you.

Old friends help you grow old, and new friends keep you young— enjoy your friends.

There is no closer friend than a beloved friend. You are a beloved friend.

Enjoy a balance of old and new friends. Old friends share a common history. They know each other's secrets and have developed a comfortable relationship that has worn well over the years. He is the friend who knew you as an awkward kid, and she is the friend who listened to all the juicy details about that important date. Old friends feel like family. New friends allow you to reinvent yourself, because they don't know what you were like in the past. They give you permission to be someone new and different and mysterious. Cultivate your friendships and appreciate the gifts they bring into your life. Whether it's an exciting new friend or a beloved buddy who knows you well, take time to nurture your friendships.

Friendships multiply joys and divide griefs.

H. G. Bohn

Friends come and friends go, but a true friend sticks by you like family.

Proverbs 18:24 MSG

Ask, and God will give you the wisdom to know what to do and when to do it.

There is a time to make things happen and a time to let things happen.

There is a perfect season for everything. Spring brings soft pink apple blossoms, but the fruit will not be ready to pick until summer has turned into fall. Little girls dress up in their mothers' shoes and clothes, pretending to be the women they will someday become. But no matter how anxious they are to grow up, maturity comes only in God's time. God's timing is always perfect. Ask for God's wisdom and guidance, and you will discover His divine timing in your life. God will show you when you are ready to step out and achieve your goals and when you need time to grow in grace and maturity. You don't have to force anything, for you can rest in God's perfect timing, and His divine seasons.

Be glad of life because it gives you the chance to love and to work and to play and to look up at the stars.

Henry Van Dyke

There is a time for everything, and a season for every activity under heaven.

Ecclesiastes 3:1 NIV

Time is a gift from God; spend it wisely, and you'll be rich in the things that count.

Yesterday is a canceled check; tomorrow is a promissory note; today is ready cash.

This moment is all you have. Yesterday is a memory, and tomorrow is only a dream, but today is the treasure you own right now. Spend the treasure of your time wisely, and you will learn to make every day a good day, no matter what the day may bring. Time is one of your most valuable, nonrenewable resources. When you relax into God's grace, you will discover that every day can be a good day. Instead of multitasking frantically or wasting time on nonessentials, focus on what is most important and meaningful to you. Take time to set your priorities. Pace yourself by also including time for rest and worship. And don't forget to set aside time to call your friends!

How you spend your time is more important than how you spend your money. Money mistakes can be corrected, but time is gone forever.

David B. Norris

Teach us to number our days aright,
that we may gain a heart of wisdom.

Psalm 90:12 NIV

Enjoy the little things, for you may one day look back and realize that they were the big things.

The little things friends shared yesterday still mean so much today.

A kind word and a loving hug, the pleasure of happy moments together, the delightful laughter of friends sharing secrets—these are small things. Yet as you look back on life, you'll discover that these are the things that really matter. You may be able to accomplish big things in the world, but it's a loving circle of friends and family who will help make those great accomplishments more meaningful. When loved ones are no longer with you, it will be the quiet memories of meaningful moments that you will treasure, not trophies on a shelf, a big house, or a promotion at work. Whether it's a cup of tea, a loving letter, or a phone call, appreciate the little things, for they are great gifts from God.

Think big thoughts but relish small pleasures.

H. Jackson Brown Jr.

A devout life does bring wealth, but it's the rich simplicity of being yourself before God.

1 Timothy 6:6 MSG

Laughter is a fountain of youth—
drink from the fountain often.

You don't stop laughing because
you grow old; you grow old
because you stop laughing.

Laughter renews your zest for life. If you've been feeling old and cranky lately, ask yourself if you've been taking things too seriously. Maybe it's time for a good old-fashioned belly laugh. God gave the gift of laughter to renew youthful spirits. Laughter helps you remember what it felt like to be as young as springtime, a laughing child, smiling at the beauties and oddities of life. Pull out old joke books and rent funny movies. Spend a few moments smiling at the antics of puppies, kittens, or anything young, awkward, and coltish. Get together with dear friends to laugh and share secrets like exuberant teenagers. Whether you are laughing through tears or with the sheer exuberance of life, remember that laughter is a fountain of youth.

> You grow up the day you have your first real laugh—at yourself.
>
> Ethel Barrymore

You have made known to me the path of life; you will fill me with joy in your presence, with eternal pleasures at your right hand.

Psalm 16:11 NIV

33

The most important things in life aren't things—they are the people you love.

A friend's loving heart is a priceless gift in life.

Sparkling diamonds and lustrous pearls, mansions, cars, and glamorous clothes all hold tremendous appeal. When you are younger, you may feel that these are the most important things in life. But how empty all those things seem if you have no one to share them with! Yet even a poor woman is rich when her loved ones surround her. Enjoy the good things that come your way, but remember that in God's kingdom, love is more important than any mere thing could ever be. Instead of buying extravagant things, be extravagant with your love. Cherish those dear to your heart, and invest time and treasure in building lasting, loving relationships. Remember that people are more important than things, and only love lasts beyond the grave.

Love one another in truth and purity, as children, impulsively, uncalculatingly.

Edward Wilson

May the Lord make your love increase and overflow for each other and for everyone else, just as ours does for you.

1 Thessalonians 3:12 NIV

35

Ask for God's wisdom and guidance,
and you will discover His divine
timing in your life.

Time is one of your most valuable,
nonrenewable resources.

Whether you are laughing through
tears or with the sheer exuberance
of life, remember that laughter
is a fountain of youth.

Every person you meet can be your teacher, if you are willing to listen and learn.

A wise person gains insights from unexpected sources.

It's easy to learn from heroes and people you agree with. You can calmly take the word of someone you admire, and those who agree with your opinions make you feel good about what you believe. But sometimes God sends other teachers into your life. He may bring important truths from unexpected and even difficult sources. Wisdom can be learned from people you may not consider wise. If you desire greater insight, learn to listen to others and see every person as a possible teacher. A difficult person may teach you lessons in patience. Someone you consider an "enemy" may offer a truth you need to hear. A child may bring a fresh perspective. Even friends can offer each other unexpected lessons.

I make it my rule to lay hold of light and embrace it, though it be held forth by a child or an enemy.

Jonathan Edwards

Jesus answered and said, "I thank You, Father, Lord of heaven and earth, that You have hidden these things from the wise and prudent and have revealed them to babes."

Matthew 11:25 NKJV

Without God's help you cannot succeed;
with God's help you cannot fail.

God is with you in every situation,
helping you reach your dreams.

God is your greatest ally. When the going gets tough, He may be your only resource. Even a friend who loves you and believes in you may only be able to cheer you from the sidelines. God is the One who will help you reach the goal. Your greatest friend and greatest helper is God. He is your never failing resource, the One who is with you in every endeavor. Take your plans, hopes, and dreams to God in prayer. Ask for His wisdom as you set your priorities. Seek His guidance every step of the way. Trust that He is using every situation to bring you closer to your goal, even when setbacks occur. God is your partner, so don't be afraid to ask for His help.

All who call on God in true faith, earnestly from the heart, will certainly be heard, and will receive what they have asked and desired.

Martin Luther

I pray for good fortune in everything you do, and for your good health—that your everyday affairs prosper, as well as your soul!

3 John 2 MSG

If you have the eyes of love, you'll see love wherever you go.

Love makes even the plainest face beautiful.

The world is a beautiful place when you see it through the eyes of love. Like a pair of rose-colored glasses, love colors the way you look at life. The lights and shadows develop a rosy glow, because love allows you to see beyond the illusions of earth and discover the heaven hidden in even the most ordinary lives. Put on the rose-colored glasses of God's love and look around you. You'll discover beauty in every human face. You can even look in the mirror and see the reflection of a face that God—and your friend—loves. You'll see that this world was created in love, and even the darkest places in the heart can be full of beauty in the light of God's love.

To love another person is to see the face of God.

Victor Hugo

The eye is the lamp of the body. If your eyes are good, your whole body will be full of light.

Matthew 6:22 NIV

*Change your thoughts, and you
can change your world.*

*Your positive thoughts and creative ideas
can make a real difference.*

Every day you are faced with decisions. You must make choices. You can choose to respond negatively or positively to the ideas and situations that God brings your way. You can be anxious about tomorrow, or you can face your future with faith. You can be closed to new ideas, or you can open your mind to embrace a larger vision. Every thought you think colors your experiences, so choose your thoughts carefully. If you believe you can make a difference, then you will find a way to do so. You can change old habits of thinking and train yourself to trust God in new ways. Like a seed planted in fertile soil, new thoughts and ideas can one day create a better way of life.

A man's mind stretched to a new idea never goes back to its original dimensions.

Oliver Wendell Holmes

Jesus said to him, "If you can believe, all things are possible to him who believes."

Mark 9:23 NKJV

*Friends know they can grow
separately without growing apart.*

*Friends share common roots, yet
give each other wings to fly.*

Friends may share a common background, but that doesn't mean they'll choose the same paths in life. One friend may stay in the hometown and raise a family, while another friend may be a globe-trotting adventurer. Yet no matter how different their lives, or how far they may wander from the family home, friends know that they can grow separately without having to grow apart. Love holds people with an open hand. As you offer each other the freedom to explore, you give love room to grow and expand. As you anchor each other in your prayers, trust grows, even though you take different paths. God watches over you. Rooted in love and respect, each friend can be free to spread her wings and soar.

> When we lose the right to be different, we lose the privilege to be free.
>
> Charles Evans Hughes

Can't you see the central issue in all this? It is not what you and I do . . . It is what God is doing, and he is creating something totally new, a free life!

Galatians 6:15 MSG

*Believe in yourself,
and others will too.*

*God is changing you
from glory into glory.*

You have a glorious destiny. God placed you here on earth for a unique purpose. Your friends also can see your potential, even when you cannot see your own abilities and talents clearly. When you believe in yourself, you believe in the strong and wonderful person God created you to be. Believe in yourself. Give yourself credit for the victories won. Give yourself grace for the losses and setbacks. Calm confidence within will be reflected in your outer life. Knowing that God is with you every step of the way, believe that you can achieve your goals, overcome your difficulties, and fulfill your unique destiny. When you have faith in yourself, then others will believe in you too, and support you as you reach for your dreams.

The only limit to our realization of tomorrow will be our doubts about today.

Franklin Delano Roosevelt

Ask in faith, never doubting, for the one who doubts is like a wave of the sea, driven and tossed by the wind.

James 1:6 NRSV

Every thought you think colors your experiences, so choose your thoughts carefully.

If you desire greater insight, learn to listen to others and see every person as a possible teacher.

God is your partner, so don't be afraid to ask for His help.

It matters less what you do and more who you are becoming by doing it.

What you become is infinitely more important than what you do or have.

Even if everyone sees you as a success, you're a failure if you have to sell your soul to achieve that success. While the world may applaud outside achievements, only you know in your heart of hearts if what you are doing aligns with your highest values. The quiet work of God in a person's heart is not dictated by what she does, but by who she is. Are you becoming a better person? Do the life you live and the work you do reflect your spiritual priorities? Every job offers an opportunity to grow in grace, but some are more suited to your spiritual growth than others. Make being a godly person your highest priority, then everything you do will glorify God.

> It's never too late to be what you might have become.
>
> George Eliot

Earn a reputation for living well in God's
eyes and the eyes of the people.

Proverbs 3:4 MSG

A small attitude adjustment can make a big difference.

If life gives you lemons, make lemonade.

When you choose a radical trust in God, you choose a new attitude toward life. Because you believe in a great God with great promises, you have every reason to choose a positive attitude, for He promises that all things work together for good for those who love Him. You can choose your attitude. You can allow fear to rule your choices. Or you can adjust your attitude and live out a fearless faith in God. Exchange your doubts for confident praise. Step out in faith, trusting that God will guide you in each choice you make. When you cannot change a situation, ask God to change you. When you choose a positive attitude of faith, it is like a compass pointing you in the right direction.

I discovered I always have choices, and sometimes it's only a choice of attitude.

Judith M. Knowlton

Be content with who you are, and don't put on airs. God's strong hand is on you; he'll promote you at the right time. Live carefree before God; he is most careful with you.

1 Peter 5:6–7 MSG

If you are patient in one moment of anger, you will escape many days of sorrow.

For every minute of anger, you lose sixty seconds of happiness.

Sometimes friends say something to provoke one another—and suddenly a childish squabble can turn into a full-blown feud. Anger adds fuel to the fire and prolongs the argument. But patience and quietness can cool the flames, giving you time to think before you speak and to make sure you won't do something you'll regret later. Learn the power of patience in the face of anger. If you struggle with anger, ask God to help you tame this emotional tiger. When you are tempted to speak first and think later, think again. Close your mouth, walk away, do whatever it takes to regain perspective. Ask God to help you calm the troubled emotional seas, and to give you His gifts of peace and patience in this situation.

He who overcomes his anger conquers his greatest enemy.

Latin Proverb

It's smart to be patient, but it's stupid to lose your temper.

Proverbs 14:29 CEV

Seek, ask, knock—and the door will open.

The only way to find out what's on the other side of the door is to walk through the open door.

It takes courage to be willing to try something new. You have to be brave enough and want it enough to make the attempt. Girls are sometimes taught to hang back, told that it isn't "ladylike" to aggressively pursue a desired goal. But from one friend to another, you are encouraged to ignore that old advice. Instead, be willing to knock on the door, ask for what you want, and search out ways to reach your goals. If you cherish a dream in your heart, you have to give it your best shot. You'll never know if you don't try. Trust God enough to put the dream to the test. Ask Him to open the doors of opportunity, and then be brave enough to walk through them.

You may be disappointed if you fail, but you are doomed if you don't try.

Beverly Sills

Ask, and you will receive. Search, and you will find.
Knock, and the door will be opened.

Matthew 7:7 CEV

You expand your perspective when you take time away to renew your spirit.

In quietness and rest you are able to hear the still small voice of God in your heart.

Do you think of shared moments of quiet renewal together? Little children walking barefoot on the sand, watching an ocean sunset. A silent hour in a quiet church, or a prayer whispered in the night. Friends quietly awed, sitting out under the stars and seeing the vastness of God's creation. You may have grown far away from childhood years where there was plenty of time for stargazing and sunsets, but you still need the nurturing and renewal that time away brings. Whether it's a beautiful place in nature or a quiet corner at home, be still long enough for God to whisper secrets of His love for you. Afterward, you will find that you have a fresh perspective and renewed strength to return to the busy life you lead.

> True silence is the rest of the mind; it is to the spirit what sleep is to the body, nourishment and refreshment.
>
> William Penn

Be still, and know that I am God.

Psalm 46:10 NIV

61

Cultivating character will grow a garden of grace and goodness.

Characters and gardens both reflect how much weeding was done in the growing season.

Character is developed over time. It is an accumulation of choices. It's like planting a garden. You decide what to put into it. You can plant seeds of patience, peace, love, and joy. You can tend the garden of your heart, uprooting the weeds of envy, anger, and fear. Whatever you cultivate will bear fruit. Whatever you weed out will make room for better things to grow. Character needs to be cultivated not only when the sun shines, but also in the rain. In all seasons, God is there to help you make the choices that build strong character; God is there to give you the strength to do your best no matter what the circumstances. Your friend sees your hard work and applauds the grace and goodness of your choices.

> The greater part of our happiness or misery depends on our disposition, and not on our circumstance.
>
> Martha Washington

The wise woman builds her house, but with her own hands the foolish one tears hers down.

Proverbs 14:1 NIV

When you choose a radical trust in God,
you choose a new attitude toward life.

Be willing to knock on the door,
ask for what you want, and search
out ways to reach your goals.

When you cannot change a situation,
ask God to change you.

Build bridges instead of burning them—you may have to cross the same river again.

Friends know how to build bridges and keep them in good repair.

Friends who want to keep their friendship close have learned the skill of building bridges instead of burning them. Instead of allowing anger or hurt feelings to separate friends, bridge builders are the first to reach out and the first to forgive. Keep your relationships in good repair. Keep in touch with a simple card or letter. If you haven't heard from a friend in a while, call and see how he or she is doing. When anger or disagreements threaten to separate friends, remember how important this person has been in your life. Ask yourself, "Do I want to lose this friendship because of a temporary disagreement?" Offer the gift of forgiveness and an open hand of friendship. Be a bridge builder, and you'll enjoy lasting and loving relationships.

> He who cannot forgive others breaks the bridge over which he himself must pass.
>
> George Herbert

How wonderful, how beautiful, when brothers and sisters get along!

Psalm 133:1 MSG

Always have something to look forward to.

*Friends look forward to sharing
good times together.*

You lead a busy and productive life. Taking care of work, family, home, and all your current obligations is a more-than-full-time job. But in the busyness of today, don't forget to plan ahead for tomorrow's good times. No matter how much there is to do, anticipating a coming pleasure can brighten your mood and help you accomplish today's tasks with zest. Start small. Set up an appointment to have coffee with friends. Mark a space in your calendar to go see that new comedy that got great reviews. Then plan something bigger, like a dream vacation. Savor the pleasure of looking forward to a well-deserved treat, and thank God for the fun when it comes. And don't forget your friend who loves to share good times with you.

> The future is as bright as the promises of God.
>
> Adoniram Judson

In alert expectancy such as this, we're never left feeling shortchanged. Quite the contrary—we can't round up enough containers to hold everything God generously pours into our lives through the Holy Spirit.

Romans 5:5 MSG

Faith is to believe what you do not see,
and its reward is to see and enjoy
what you believe.

The fruit of faith is the
fulfillment of your hope.

You don't have to make giant leaps of faith. Baby steps will do. You didn't mature from a child into an adult overnight, so why would you expect to gain spiritual maturity in an instant? God leads you along gently, one step of faith at a time. Faith is both a gift and a choice. God shows you the path that faith requires, but you are the one who chooses to take the next step. As you grow in faith, you'll find you have more opportunities to trust and demonstrate faith. As one prayer is answered, you develop the confidence to pray for more. As one step of faith leads to fulfillment, you'll have the courage to take another, larger step in God's direction.

I learned really to practice mustard seed faith, and positive thinking, and remarkable things happened.

John Walton

With God nothing will be impossible.

Luke 1:37 NKJV

There is one thing in the world really worth pursuing—knowing God.

May you find delight and joy worshiping in God's presence.

Many people talk about God, but few really know Him intimately. You can usually recognize the ones who do have a close relationship with God. They don't need to talk about it, and they don't have a lot of formulaic answers. They just quietly radiate His love. It's as if by drawing closer to God, they begin to reflect His qualities in their lives. Take time to get to know God more intimately. Set aside time for prayer, and when you pray, spend some of that time just worshiping, basking in His presence, and thanking Him for the gifts He brings into your life. As you draw closer to God, you'll discover an inner peace and hidden springs of joy that blesses friends, family, and a friend who loves you.

A little knowledge of God is worth a lot more than a great deal of knowledge about him.

J. I. Packer

Let us know, let us press on to know the LORD; his appearing is as sure as the dawn; he will come to us like showers, like the spring rains that water the earth.

Hosea 6:3 NRSV

Ensure that you'll be adaptable in old age by being flexible while you are still young.

You are only as old as you think you are.

Young children have supple young bodies that move with a coltish ease and grace. They also have supple minds, open to new ideas and limitless possibilities. As you grow older, it's easy to lose track of that youthful agility and sense of wonder. But youth is as much a matter of spirit as of body, and a person can choose to be mature without becoming old and rigid. Make a deliberate choice to be flexible in body and mind. Take a class that stretches you—whether it's an exercise class or learning a new skill. Keep your mind open to new ideas and be receptive to the wonders of God's creation. Renew your acquaintance with childlike laughter and heartfelt secrets. Cultivate flexibility in your life, and discover youthful joy again.

What you and I become in the end will be more and more of what we are deciding and trying to be right now.

John Powell

As for me, I trust in You, O LORD; I say, "You are my God."
My times are in Your hand.

Psalm 31:14–15 NKJV

Remember, a bend in the road is not the end of the road.

God has wonderful surprises for you—just around the corner.

Life's path seemed to spread out ahead of
you like a golden highway shining in the sun.
But then an unexpected detour stopped you in
your tracks. Losses, layoffs, deaths, sudden
changes—life takes its toll, and you begin to
be afraid that the golden highway of life has
turned into a dark and dangerous dead end.
But God didn't bring you this far to let you
down. This is just a bend in the road, not the
end of the road. You may not know what's
around the next corner, but you know who is
walking with you. Take God's hand and let Him
lead you step-by-step back into the sunlight.
And remember that your friend is cheering you
on, every step of the way.

In a higher world
it is otherwise,
but here below
to live is to
change, and to
be perfect is to
change often.

John Henry Newman

We walk by faith, not by sight.

2 Corinthians 5:7 NKJV

You have the grace within to deal with the challenges without.

God gives you the grace you need one moment at a time.

You have a secret spring within your heart. It is the hidden gift of God's grace, springing up like an ever-flowing fountain, a deep well that will quench your thirst when life seems like a desert. Moment by moment, that gentle grace sustains you through every trouble and trial, and through all the changes of a lifetime. When you feel overwhelmed, take time to drink from the gentle springs of God's ever-refreshing grace. Rely on this inner strength to help you deal with the challenges of daily life. See God's grace in the faces of family and loved ones, too. It might come in the form of a caring friend or an unexpected opportunity, but grace will appear in your life just when you need it most.

Your worst days are never so bad that you are beyond the reach of God's grace. And your best days are never so good that you are beyond the need of God's grace.

Jerry Bridges

My grace is sufficient for you, for power
is made perfect in weakness.

2 Corinthians 12:9 NRSV

Be a bridge builder, and you'll enjoy
lasting and loving relationships.

Keep your mind open to new ideas, and be
receptive to the wonders of God's creation.

Savor the pleasure of looking forward
to a well-deserved treat, and thank
God for the fun when it comes.

*Life is a feast. Don't miss out
on any of the courses.*

Enjoy every delicious moment of your life.

A little girl embraces life fully and without reservation. Watch a child eat an ice-cream cone, and you'll see a picture of life being savored with every fiber of her being. Don't allow yourself to lose that love of life. Life is a feast, and every moment offers something unique to savor. Embrace your life with open arms and be willing to try every dish God sets before you. Enjoy the exotic flavors of new experiences and different cultures. Savor the homegrown joys of family. Taste the joy of laughter with buddies, and let salty tears of sadness be wiped away by a friend who shares your sorrow. Thank God for the feast of life and let His joy fill your heart, season by season, dish by dish.

A cheerful look makes a dish a feast.

George Herbert

You prepare a table before me in the presence of my enemies; you anoint my head with oil; my cup overflows.

Psalm 23:5 NRSV

If you believe things will work out, you'll see opportunities instead of obstacles.

It's all in the way you look at it.

What do you really believe? When you are faced with an obstacle, do you truly trust that God can help you work things out and that you are up to the challenge? If you keep telling yourself "I can't do this," then you'll live down to your own expectations of yourself. Rehearsing worst-case scenarios and disasters in your head can help create the very thing you fear. Make a deliberate choice to believe that an obstacle is nothing more than that—an obstacle that you can overcome, because you are entirely capable of reaching your goal. Concentrate on the results you want, as an athlete focuses on the goal she's reaching for. Remember that obstacles can become opportunities, with a little self-confidence and some help from God.

If you think you can, you can. If you think you can't, you're right.

Mary Kay Ash

You know that under pressure, your faith-life is forced into the open and shows its true colors.

James 1:3 MSG

Remove failure as an option, and your chances for success become infinitely better.

Success comes in cans;
failure comes in can'ts.

In the eyes of your loving friend, you are
already a success. Yet you still have goals you
want to achieve, dreams you want to see come
true. In your quest for success, remember that
setbacks are not failures, and those things that
others label as "failure" can be life lessons that
help you reach your goals eventually, if you're
willing to learn from them. You are a failure
only if you call yourself one. Failure comes
when you quit, when you say "I can't." Saying
"I can't" is just another way of saying "I
won't." There is always something to be
gained from the experience of reaching for the
stars. No matter what happens, God sees you
as a success because you did your best.

> All things are
> possible once
> you make
> them so.
>
> Wolfgang von
> Goethe

Commit to the LORD whatever you do, and your plans will succeed.

Proverbs 16:3 NIV

Every obstacle you overcome is a stepping-stone on the path to greatness.

Trying times are no time to quit trying.

Who is crazy enough to think that overcoming obstacles is fun? Well, the athlete, for one. An athlete actually loves the obstacles and trains herself to reach the goal she has set, whether it is breaking a record, leaping a hurdle, or winning a competition. A weight lifter wants to lift heavier weights, for the heavier weights build muscle and strength. You can take a tip from these athletes and see obstacles as stepping-stones that bring out your inner greatness. It can feel wonderful to test your strength against the world. You learn a lot about yourself—who you are and what you are made of. With God helping you and your friends cheering you on, you can celebrate your strength in overcoming obstacles and achieving your goals.

> You have set yourselves a difficult task, but you will succeed if you persevere; and you will find joy in overcoming obstacles.
>
> Helen Keller

Keep on being brave! It will bring you great rewards.
Learn to be patient, so that you will please God
and be given what he has promised.

Hebrews 10:35–36 CEV

Courage is like a muscle—
it is strengthened by use.

Your courage inspires your friends to
make strong and courageous choices.

It takes courage to stand up for yourself. Every time you do, you make it that much easier to make the courageous choice again. Every time you run away from a confrontation, it becomes harder to confront the next difficult situation. Each courageous choice strengthens your character, just as a muscle is strengthened by being used. The courageous choice sets you free, encouraging you to continue to live by your truth instead of trying to please or placate others. When your knees knock together and your heart beats faster, remember that God is there to give you the courage you need. Whether you are facing an outer adversary or an inner fear, remember that your courageous choice can be an inspiration to others as well as to yourself.

Courage faces fear and thereby masters it; cowardice represses fear and is thereby mastered by it.

Martin Luther King Jr.

With [God] on my side I'm fearless, afraid of no one and nothing.

Psalm 27:1 MSG

91

Creativity is a gift from God, and using your creativity is your gift to God.

Have the courage to start something new, learn something new, enjoy something new.

You are creative—a wonderfully unique and gifted person. Your friend can appreciate that creativity and enjoy watching you blossom as you cultivate your creative potential. Your God-given talents and gifts are hints from the Creator that you have a special work to do on earth. It is a work that no one else can do, and if you don't do it, then that wonderful potential will never be realized. Nurture your creativity. Pay special attention to the things that kindle your interest, and understand that a creative passion can become a wonderful and inspiring expression of the Creator who made you as you are. Practice your creative skills as a gift to God, fashioning a better world with your mind and hands and heart. Be courageously creative.

God has given each of us our "marching orders." Our purpose here on earth is to find these orders and carry them out. Those orders acknowledge our special gifts.

Søren Kierkegaard

We are His workmanship, created in Christ Jesus for good works, which God prepared beforehand that we should walk in them.

Ephesians 2:10 NKJV

Remember that obstacles can become opportunities, with a little self-confidence and some help from God.

There is always something to be gained from the experience of reaching for the stars.

Life is a feast, and every moment offers something unique to savor.

*Give others something you'd like
to receive yourself, and you'll
receive greater joy in giving.*

God loves and rewards a cheerful giver.

A gift from the heart is priceless. When you give something that is important and desirable to you, it carries a piece of your heart. These kinds of gifts express your personality and make the gift unique. The person receiving the gift feels loved and valued because you cared enough to give the very best. It's not just things that count. Giving your time and talents can touch a heart and draw giver and receiver closer together. Give the gift of yourself. Spend time with a friend or a loved one, or offer small loving services such as a back rub or pet-sitting. You are a gift to your friend, as well. God rewards you richly when you share the gift of yourself.

A cheerful giver does not count the cost of what he gives. His heart is set on pleasing and cheering him to whom the gift is given.

Julian of Norwich

If you give to others, you will be given a full amount in return. It will be packed down, shaken together, and spilling over into your lap. The way you treat others is the way you will be treated.

Luke 6:38 CEV

*If you want to lift yourself up,
lift up someone else.*

*There is no exercise better for the
heart than reaching down and
lifting someone else up.*

When life seems discouraging and you're tempted to feel sorry for yourself, that's the time to reach out to someone else. Instead of allowing a blue mood to rule, brighten up another person's day. Your encouraging word and helping hand will mean more than you know. Start with friends. Is someone you know feeling low? Your sympathetic ear and caring heart can lift your friend's spirits and make her day better. Then expand your giving. Volunteer to help at a local charity or join a workday with an organization close to your heart. Sharing others' burdens helps to put your own troubles into perspective. You can have fun, help people in need, and lift your own spirits by reaching out to others.

> Every charitable act is a stepping stone toward heaven.
>
> Henry Ward Beecher

Whoever gives one of these little ones only a cup of cold water in the name of a disciple, assuredly, I say to you, he shall by no means lose his reward.

Matthew 10:42 NKJV

*The time is always right
to do what is right.*

You inspire others by your good example.

Mothers tell their children, "Be a good example." To youthful ears, that sounds pretty boring. Exciting daredevils, glamorous beauty queens, or fabulously popular winners sound like much more fun. But Mom really does know best, and a good example is far more inspiring in the long run than winning popularity contests. Doing right may sound simple, but it's not always easy. Sometimes it will be the hardest thing you ever do. There may be no glamour or excitement in being honest, doing good work, and staying true to your ideals. But there will be the glow of accomplishment and an inner peace. With God's help, you can choose a life of integrity. When you choose to honor your highest values, you are a living inspiration to all.

> A good example is like a bell that calls many to church.
>
> Danish Proverb

Slack habits and sloppy work are as bad as vandalism.

Proverbs 18:9 MSG

When you understand that self-worth is not determined by net worth, you'll enjoy financial freedom.

If you want to feel rich, just count all the things you have that money can't buy.

It would be fun to have a million dollars, wouldn't it? Think of all the things you could buy and the places you could go. But you don't need money to prove you are special or to build up your self-image. When it comes to being a lovable person, you have everything you need, just as you are. Don't allow your net worth to determine your self-worth. Remember that you are already rich in the things money can't buy. Money is no substitute for character or for staying true to your dreams or for bringing joy to a friend who loves and admires you. Keep putting your trust in the God who loves you and who will always be your supply. Remember that you never need to buy anyone's approval.

> There is nothing wrong with people possessing riches. The wrong comes when riches possess people.
>
> Billy Graham

He is like a tree planted by streams of water, which yields its fruit in season and whose leaf does not wither. Whatever he does prospers.

Psalm 1:3 NIV

Nothing is so strong as gentleness, and nothing so gentle as real strength.

True strength comes from within and can move mountains.

The television wrestler pounds his chest and flexes his muscles, declaring he's the greatest of them all and that he'll pound his opponent into the ground. Such loudmouthed bragging seems rather silly when you compare it to real strength. True strength comes from a quiet gentleness that is compassionate and sensitive to others. Quiet strength is exhibited in the iron will of a person who stands for something she believes in, even when others are trying to shout her down. It's demonstrated by a mother caring for a sick daughter, a friend defending another friend from bullies, and a hero who triumphs over temptation. Remember this beautiful picture of God's strength: a gentle Shepherd who is strong enough to fight wolves yet watches over His sheep with tender care.

> How sweet it is when the strong are also gentle!
>
> Libbie Fudim

The wisdom that comes from heaven is first of all pure; then peace-loving, considerate, submissive, full of mercy and good fruit, impartial and sincere.

James 3:17 NIV

Today's preparation determines tomorrow's achievement.

Failing to prepare is preparing to fail.

Make your plans, do your best, and trust God with the rest. It's all in the preparation. A young soprano's bravura performance comes from years of study and hours of practice. An Olympic gold medal is won by disciplined workouts and by playing the game. Whatever your goal may be, the planning you do today will prepare you for tomorrow's success. Making a long-term plan is one way to prepare the way for success. Break it into step-by-step tasks, deciding how long it will take to do each step. Do something toward that goal every day, even if it's only making a phone call or jotting down a list of things to do. Because you're willing to prepare, your friend will be able to applaud your success.

> Planning is bringing the future into the present so you can do something about it now.
>
> Alan Lakein

We plan the way we want to live, but only
GOD makes us able to live it.

Proverbs 16:9 MSG

God rewards you richly when you share the gift of yourself.

Your sympathetic ear and caring heart can lift your friend's spirits and make her day better.

When you choose to honor your highest values, you are a living inspiration to all.

Find a job you love, and you'll never have to work a day in your life.

Pleasure in the job puts perfection in the work.

If you love to do something, it doesn't feel like work, even if you work hard doing it. As a child, you dreamed of growing up and doing something wonderful. As an adult, finding your life work may be more complex. If you're in a job that's more work than pleasure, perhaps you need to reconnect with childhood dreams and find something closer to your heart's desire. When you love what you do, you do your work well. You put energy and passion into every task, even the repetitive and mundane work. Though you may not have a "perfect" job, you can take pleasure in work well done. Ask God to help you love the job you have while you're looking for a job you'll love.

Nothing is work unless you'd rather be doing something else.

George Halas

Observe people who are good at their work—skilled workers are always in demand and admired.

Proverbs 22:29 MSG

When you look in the mirror, you're looking at someone God loves.

Remember that your friend loves you too.

Her image stares back at you from the looking glass. That familiar face is loved by family and friends. But sometimes you have trouble loving the person you see in the mirror. It's easy to see a distorted picture of yourself through eyes that criticize and judge. Take another look. See yourself, not with the eyes of judgment or criticism, but with the eyes of love—God's love. In God's eyes, the person in the mirror is beautiful: perfect and complete, cherished and beloved. God forgives your faults, understands your struggles, and accepts you completely, just as you are. God sees not only what you are now, but what you are going to be. So when you see your reflection in a mirror, remember that God loves you.

Christianity is about acceptance, and if God accepts me as I am, then I had better do the same.

Hugh Montefiore

The LORD your God is with you, he is mighty to save.
He will take great delight in you, he will quiet you
with his love, he will rejoice over you with singing.

Zephaniah 3:17 NIV

There is no danger of developing eyestrain when you look on the bright side of things.

Look on the bright side, for God's loving care is as sure as sunlight.

Pollyanna is an old-fashioned girlhood story that still resonates with modern women. She was the little girl who played the "glad game" and who looked for the silver lining behind every cloud. Whenever people want to heap scorn on someone they think is being unrealistically optimistic, they'll call her a "Pollyanna." But Pollyanna knew the secret of living well, and even modern medical science is proving that a positive outlook creates better physical health. The next time you find yourself walking in the shadows, make a decision to cross over to the sunny side of the street. Just as you can look in the mirror and see the face of someone God loves, look at your life and see the place where God is working miracles.

> Optimism is the faith that leads to achievement. Nothing can be done without hope and confidence.
>
> Helen Keller

The LORD God is a sun and shield; the LORD bestows favor and honor; no good thing does he withhold from those whose walk is blameless.

Psalm 84:11 NIV

115

Base your life on God's truth, for the truth has the power to set you free.

The desire for truth is the desire for God.

Friends tell each other the truth. They know that even a little white lie can tie a relationship in knots and create hurt and angry feelings. Building a life on lies and half-truths is like building on shifting sands. But the truth stands like a rock, unmoving and dependable. Telling the truth is one aspect of truth. But there is a greater truth—the truth of God's love. God is the source of truth and helps you face your own truth. If you have the courage to look into the face of God and see His forgiveness and love, then you will have the courage to admit when you haven't been truthful with yourself or with others. When you speak the truth, you will be set free.

We know the truth, not only by reason, but also by the heart.

Blaise Pascal

You will know the truth, and the truth will set you free.

John 8:32 NIV

Success is how high you bounce when you hit bottom.

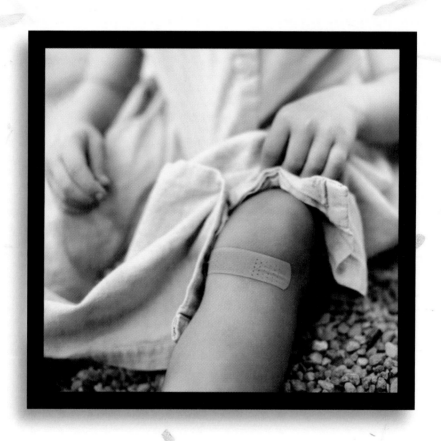

The harder the conflict, the more glorious the triumph.

It hurts to fall down. A little girl who falls off her bicycle can be comforted with hugs and bandages, then encouraged to get back on her bicycle. Eventually she learns that falling down doesn't stop her from tasting the triumph of riding that bicycle all the way around the block. You're an adult now, but the lesson from learning to ride a bike still holds true. You may face some hard times as you try to build a career, nurture a family, or create a project. Sometimes there will be setbacks. But with God's grace, you can begin again. And when you finally achieve that success you worked so hard and long for, the triumph will be even sweeter because of all you have survived and overcome.

Success is to be measured not so much by the position that one has reached in life as by the obstacles he has overcome trying to succeed.

Booker T. Washington

In times of trouble, God is with us, and when we are knocked down, we get up again.

2 Corinthians 4:9 CEV

Happiness depends on what happens;
joy is a gift from God.

The joy of the Lord is your strength,
and friends share that joy together.

Happiness comes from being asked to the prom or finding a shiny new bicycle under the Christmas tree. It depends on whether or not you got that promotion, how you feel in a new suit, or the bonus check that means you can afford a special vacation. But seasons change, and instead of sunny skies, rain falls. A devastating loss, illness, and difficult times seem to bring no reason to rejoice. That's when you need to go to the source and find your joy in the Lord instead of in circumstances. He will be your comforter and provider. Even in the darkest night, He can bring joy in the morning. Then you will discover that not only does God bring you joy, but He also gives you enough to share with others.

Joy is the most infallible sign of the presence of God.

Leon Bloy

Ask and you will receive, and your joy will be complete.

John 16:24 NIV

The will of God will never take you where the grace of God cannot keep you.

The center of God's will is the safest place you can be.

If your friend could wrap her arms around you and protect you from all problems and sorrows in life, she would. But no matter how much friends love one another, only God can see them through life's changes and challenges. God is with both, sheltering each under His great umbrella of grace and love. No matter where you go or what you do, you will be in the center of God's grace. His love surrounds you and enfolds you and carries you through every circumstance. He will never leave you or forsake you. Praise God for His grace, lift your hands, and rejoice in His love. And remember that you have a friend who loves you and prays for your peace and happiness.

There is nothing but God's grace. We walk upon it; we breathe it; we live and die by it; it makes the nails and the axles of the universe.

Robert Louis Stevenson

From his fullness we have all received, grace upon grace.

John 1:16 NRSV

God sees not only what you are now,
but what you are going to be.

If you're in a job that's more work than
pleasure, perhaps you need to reconnect
with childhood dreams and find something
closer to your heart's desire.

Look at your life and see the place where
God is working miracles.

Friendships multiply joys and divide griefs.

H. G. Bohn

Friends come and friends go, but a true friend
sticks by you like family.

Proverbs 18:24 MSG